Community Places

by Tyrone Parker

National Geographic and the Yellow Border are registered trademarks of the National Geographic Society.

National Geographic School Publishing
Hampton-Brown
www.NGSP.com

Printed in the USA.
RR Donnelley, Johnson City, TN

ISBN: 978-0-7362-7993-2

11 12 13 14 15 16 17 18 19   10 9 8 7 6 5 4

Acknowledgments and credits continue on the inside back cover.

This is a bakery.

bread

She can get her bread.

This is a grocery store.

cereal

She can get her cereal.

This is a restaurant.

soup

She can get her soup.

This is her house.
She can get a hug!